REEFS

By Ruth Radlauer and Henry M. Anderson

Photographs by Henry M. Anderson

A Radlauer Geo Book

AN ELK GROVE BOOK

 CHILDRENS PRESS, CHICAGO

**Created for Childrens Press
by Radlauer Productions, Incorporated**

Henry M. Anderson, a graduate in marine biology
from the University of North Carolina at Wilmington, is
a Park Ranger/Naturalist at Virgin Islands National
Park, where he lives with his wife and son.

Photo credits:
Australian Tourist Commission, page 16
Virgin Islands National Park, page 36
Diagram page 10 by Rolf Zillmer

Cover: Squirrelfish and Coral

Library of Congress Cataloging in Publication Data

Radlauer, Ruth Shaw.
  Reefs.
    (A Radlauer geo book)
    "An Elk Grove book."
    Includes index.
    Summary: Explores the rigid, wave-resistant struc-
ture formed by skeletons of corals, which provides a
favorable environment for the symbiotic existence of
marine plants and animals.
    1. Coral reef biology — Juvenile literature.
[1. Coral reef biology. 2. Coral reef ecology.
3. Ecology] I. Anderson, Henry M., ill. II. Title.
III. Series.
QH95.8.R33 1983   574.5'26367   82-17862
ISBN 0-516-07836-4

  2 3 4 5 6 7 8 9 10 11 12 13 14 15 R 89 88 87 86 85 84

CONTENTS

What is this dark, mysterious pla e where colorful fish glide among strange formations? it's a reef, a ridge under the water. Some reefs are made of rock and sand. But this is a coral reef formed by billions of tiny animals that grow together in clumps called colonies.

WHAT IS A REEF?

A coral reef means different things to different people. A **geologist** looks at a coral reef as one of earth's many life processes that makes a rigid, wave resistant formation out of the skeletons of tiny marine animals like the coral **polyp**.

When **ecologists** look at a coral reef, they see marine plants and animals living together in an environmental community. Each type of animal has a role in the **food chain**: **producer**, **consumer**, or **decomposer**.

Nature lovers see the reef as a wonder of marine life, color, and change. For a diver, it's a soft, mysterious place where he or she can see, hear, and be close to the creatures that live on the coral reef.

geologist
　　scientist who studies earth's history as recorded in rocks and formations

polyp
　　wormlike animal whose secretions form the hard surfaces of the coral

ecologist
　　scientist who studies relationships between plants and animals and their environment

food chain
　　the order in which organisms in a community feed on each other, beginning with plants, eaten by plant eaters which are eaten by meat eaters that may be eaten by larger meat eaters

producer
　　plant or animal that creates food

consumer
　　animal that eats other life forms

decomposer
　　organism that changes matter into a form usable by other life forms

With careful instruction and a lot of practice, you can join the fish that swim through the underwater world of a coral reef.

REEF EXPLORING

Since you aren't a fish, you'll have to **snorkel** or **scuba dive** to explore a reef. A snorkel tube allows you to breathe as you swim along the surface with your face in the water. You use a face mask to help you see without the blur caused by water against your eyes. Fins on your feet propel you through the water and assist you when you want to go deeper. But, of course, you won't go deeper until you've mastered the skill of clearing water from your snorkel tube when you come up for air.

Scuba divers don't need to come up for air as often. They carry air tanks on their backs. A pressure gauge tells how much air is left in the tank. A diver knows when it's time to come out of the water.

If you learn snorkeling and scuba diving from **qualified instructors**, practice a long time under supervision, and follow other rules listed on page 41, you'll have the privilege of getting to know a coral reef.

snorkel
> to swim with mask, breathing tube, and fins

scuba dive
> to swim under water with self-contained underwater breathing apparatus *(scuba)* which includes air tank, regulators, mask, and gauges

qualified instructor
> usually a person trained and certified by one of the national associations (See Glossary)

Turtle Grass Field

Sea Cucumber

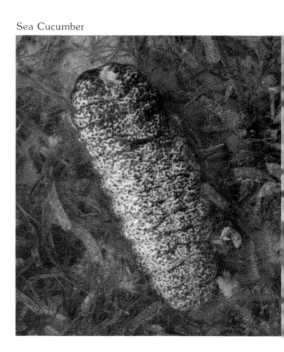

Even if you can't go under water, the seashore
near a reef is worth exploring.

SEASHORE RAMBLES

If you are not a swimmer, you can still enjoy the seashore. Quite often, you will find shallow, rocky areas and **turtle grass** flats waiting to be explored.

You need old tennis shoes to protect your feet from sharp rocks, dead or live coral, and sea urchins. And since the sun's rays are very strong, even on cloudy days, you'll wear a shirt and maybe long pants to prevent sunburn.

Turtle grass is named for the sea turtles that feed on animals sheltered in the grass. On a stroll through turtle grass, you may discover a piece of coral. Slowly lift it and you'll see crabs, urchins, and sponges at home. Even after the coral is dead, it still provides a home for hundreds of other animals.

Pieces of live and dead coral are broken up into small bits by boring animals and pounding waves. When at last they are washed ashore, these tiny particles form the beautiful white coral sands along the shore.

turtle grass
> a flowering plant that grows in shallow water and forms underwater meadows

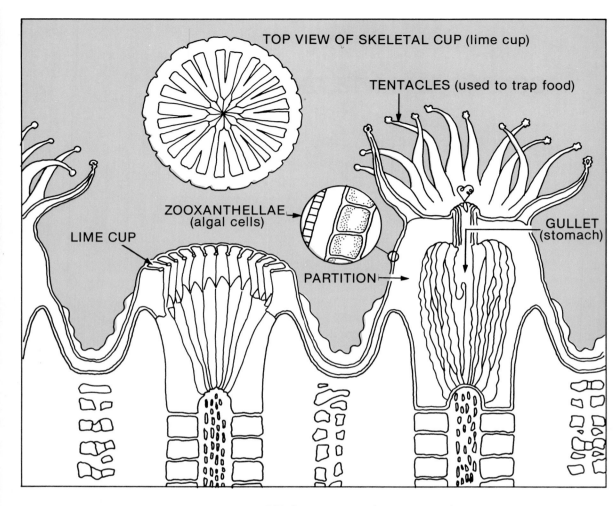

TOP VIEW OF SKELETAL CUP (lime cup)

TENTACLES (used to trap food)

ZOOXANTHELLAE (algal cells)

LIME CUP

GULLET (stomach)

PARTITION

DIAGRAM OF A POLYP. With its tentacles, a coral polyp reaches out at night to trap food and bring it to the gullet, or mouth. Food passes into a cavity, or hole, where food is digested. The polyp's wormlike body forms a protective outer skeleton known as a **lime** cup.

CORALS—PLANTS OR ANIMALS?

Plants and animals are grouped according to their special characteristics. Some animal groupings are birds, fish, reptiles, and mammals.

The reef is home for many groups of animals found only in this special place. One such animal is coral, which is made up of a colony of small polyps. Each polyp is a tiny, worm-shaped animal that **secretes** a material called **calcium carbonate**. This calcium carbonate hardens into a **lime** cup around the polyp's soft body. The hard material formed over many years by millions of polyps makes a special pattern or shape like that of brain coral or tube coral.

A coral feeds by extending its **tentacles** out of its lime cup into the surrounding water. The coral waits patiently for the microscopic sea life called plankton to brush against its tentacles which are lined with stinging cells that paralyze the **prey**. The prey is then quickly passed by the tentacles to the mouth and digested.

secretes
  pushes liquid through the surface — An organism pushes liquid through its surface.
calcium carbonate (CaCO$_3$)
  material taken from sea water by some sea animals to form a hard, protective cover, shell, or skeleton
lime
  calcium carbonate
tentacles
  armlike extensions that capture prey
prey
  animal caught and eaten by another animal, or predator

This brain coral gets its color from the algae living within its cells. The relationship between coral and algae is an interesting one.

SYMBIOSIS

Growing within some corals are single-celled **algae**. In a relationship called **symbiosis**, the coral benefits from oxygen and **nutrients** given off by the algae. The algae benefit from having a well-protected home in the tissues of the coral where they recycle the coral's waste to make food. And since all plants need **carbon dioxide** (CO_2), a gas given off by all animals, the algae use that CO_2 along with sunlight and water to perform their **photosynthesis**.

algae
> (singular *alga*) water plants which have no true roots, stems, leaves, or flowers — Algae are grouped according to color.

symbiosis
> relationship between two organisms in which each benefits from the other

nutrients
> things that help a plant or animal grow or repair itself

carbon dioxide (CO_2)
> heavy, colorless, odorless gas

photosynthesis
> process by which plants use light, water, and CO_2 to produce food

Just like plants in a garden, corals need a special balance of water, sunlight, and correct temperature. Although this tube coral hides in dark places, it seems to burst with fiery sunshine.

FRAGILE! ENJOY GENTLY

Corals are usually found in warm, **tropical** oceans where they have all the right conditions for healthy growth. They do best when the water has a **salinity** of about 35% and a temperature above 21° **C** (70° **F**). Because 50 meters of water filter out most of the sun's rays, most corals cannot grow below that depth.

Corals are fragile. They cannot live where fresh water runs off the land into the ocean. Polluted water also damages coral reefs because it destroys the balance of salt, **oxygen**, and other things needed for growth.

Reefs are endangered by careless snorkelers who bump or stand on them. Even touching a coral can leave it scarred and more open to disease.

Corals grow very slowly, some only 5 or 7.5 centimeters (2 or 3 inches) a year. Breaking off a piece of coral by accident or on purpose spoils the beauty of the reef. A good motto for underwater people might be, "Enjoy gently."

tropical
    located in the tropics (near equator)
salinity
    saltiness
C
    Celsius or centigrade; metric temperature scale with freezing at 0° and boiling at 100°
F
    Fahrenheit; nonmetric temperature scale with freezing at 32° and boiling at 212°
oxygen
    element present in air and water; invisible gas needed for life

Butterfly Fish

Most reef formations are combinations of many
different types of coral and other marine animals and
plants. The Great Barrier Reef near Australia is a huge
home for countless animals like this butterfly fish,
corals, and other sea life.

REEF FORMATIONS

There are three major types of coral reefs in the world. Fringing reefs start growing on rocks along the shore. The reef gradually grows out toward the sea with most of the growth taking place at the outer edges. This type of reef is very common and makes it easy for snorkelers to find good places to explore close to shore.

An atoll is a circle of coral reef often built on the crater rim of an ancient volcano. This type of circular or crescent-shaped island reef is common in the Pacific Ocean, and there are atolls in the **Caribbean Sea**.

A barrier reef forms parallel to the shoreline. It's similar to a fringing reef but big enough and long enough to form a **lagoon** between the reef and the beach. The world's largest reef of this kind is the Great Barrier Reef off the northeastern coast of Australia.

These different kinds of reefs form because of shoreline shapes and the direction the shore faces. Wind, waves, currents, seashore drainage, and even bottom **sediment** also affect a reef's formation.

Caribbean Sea
    body of water between Central America and the Atlantic Ocean
lagoon
    shallow body of water between narrow strip of land and the shore; also the sheltered body of water on the inside of an atoll
sediment
    solid matter that settles to the bottom of liquid

Elkhorn Coral

The big, strong elkhorn coral protects more delicate corals from pounding waves. Most of the animal **species** shown in this book are found in the Caribbean Sea. Other species of the same animals are found in other places of the world.

TYPES OF CORAL

Many plants and animals have two names. One is a common name that people give to them. For example, a coral with long flat blades resembling an elk's antlers was named elkhorn coral. When **marine biologists** classified this coral, they gave it a scientific name, or **nomenclature**, *Acropora palmata*.

Elkhorn coral is one of the largest, most common corals. The elkhorn is usually found on the outer edge of a reef in the **surf zone**. This coral is massive, so it protects much of the reef by absorbing some of the heavy wave action that would otherwise break smaller, fragile corals.

Staghorn coral *(Acropora cervicornis)* looks a lot like a **stag's** antlers. It lives in quiet water where it grows about five to six inches a year. Both elkhorn and staghorn corals are very important because they provide shelter for reef fish.

species
    living organisms which have special features that only their group has
marine biologist
    scientist who studies plants and animals of the sea
nomenclature
    standardized names given to plants and animals by scientists, usually in Classical Latin or Greek
surf zone
    area where ocean waves break and form surf
stag
    male deer

Saucer coral *(Helioseris cucullata)* is small and fragile. It's usually found under ledges or nestled between larger corals.

MORE CORALS

Saucer coral is only as big as a young person's hand, but it's amazingly beautiful. It has ruffled ridges, usually tinted green by the single-celled algae that live in its tissues. A watchful snorkeler can easily spot this coral that looks so much like lettuce.

Brain coral *(Diploria labrinthiformis)* is probably the easiest of all the corals to identify because the surface looks like an animal's brain. Growing very slowly, brain coral can reach the size of a boulder. Because of its huge size, it is a tempting resting place for a tired snorkeler in shallow water. But standing on a brain coral kills its surface and leaves the top scarred and unhealthy.

Brain coral often serves as a cleaning station. Living directly on the surface of this coral are small fish called cleaner gobies *(Gobiosoma genie)*. The cleaner goby is just one of many **organisms** that get food by cleaning **parasites** from the scales of other fish.

organism
  any living thing
parasite
  organism that takes nourishment from another living thing

Unidentified Coral

Fire Coral

Scientists are calling the fantastic animal at the top an "unidentified coral." The other one shown is an "unfriendly cousin" called fire coral.

CORAL "COUSINS"

Soft corals make up another animal group found on a reef. They resemble plants because they are anchored to the sea bottom and have soft, often feathery branches that sway with the ocean currents.

Anemones are sometimes called "flowers of the sea," even though they are really animals. Anemones are closely related to corals. Just as corals do, they trap their food by stinging prey with their tentacles.

Fire corals are not true corals, but are closely related to the jelly fish known as the Portuguese Man-Of-War. Brushing against a fire coral will give you a burning sensation similar to sunburn. The fire coral is difficult to recognize because it grows in a variety of shapes. It can be bladelike and branched or flat and encrusted with tiny, hairlike fingers. A diver can sometimes distinguish this nuisance from true coral by its mustard orange color and smooth appearance.

Sponge

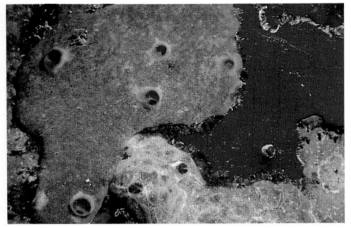

Sponges

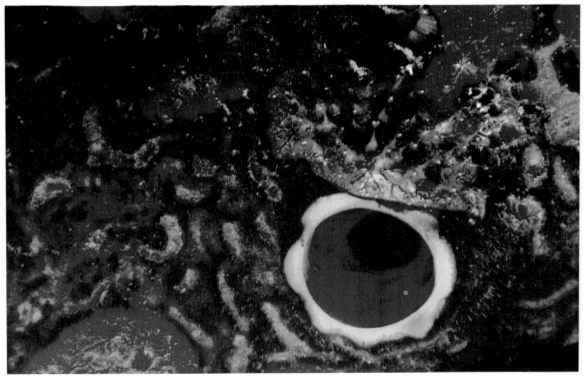

Sponges are among the most colorful of reef
inhabitants. Long thought to be a plant, the sponge is
really an animal.

SPONGES

Are sponges plants or animals? Even scientists were confused by these organisms for many years. At first sponges were classified as plants. They are often plantlike with branched or tubular parts. They are simple in structure and anchored to the bottom of the sea. But sponges are not plants.

A sponge is a colony of animal cells. It feeds by creating a current with its cells which have tiny fringes of hair called cilia that flutter back and forth. The fluttering of the cilia draws water into the sponge which then **filters** out the plankton for food.

Sponges are like miniature "hotels." Their narrow passageways and cavities serve as ideal homes for small shrimp, crabs, and **brittlestars**. A large sponge can have hundreds of such residents hiding inside it.

filter
> to strain or trap food from the water

brittlestar
> spindly-legged echinoderm — See page 33.

Flat Worm

Christmas Tree Worm

Feather Duster Worm

Not all worms are in the garden, nor are they all
long and slithery. Some marine worms are flat. Others
are shaped like Christmas trees and feather dusters.

WORMS

A worm is a worm. Right? Not when you discover the worms that live on a coral reef. **Marine** worms hardly resemble earthworms at all. Nestled among the corals of a reef are fan worms *(Sabellastarte magnifica)* and Christmas tree worms *(Spirobranchus giganteus)*. The Christmas tree worm is a small, delicately spiraled wonder that comes in a variety of colors.

Try touching a Christmas tree or fan worm. As soon as you get close, it disappears before your eyes with lightning speed. The worms actually withdraw into their tubes for protection. After a few minutes they expand their feathery extensions to breathe and to trap and filter food from the water.

Watch out for the bristle worm *(Hermodice carunculata)*. It looks like a harmless white caterpillar, but if you touch it, the bristles stick in your skin. The worm's self defense can create a painful problem for a curious person.

marine
    of the sea

Banded Coral Shrimp

Whenever you snorkel or scuba dive on a coral reef, stop and listen. The background noise you hear is a chorus of lobsters, shrimp, crabs, and fish making chirps. whistles, clicks, rasps, and grunts.

SHRIMP AND OTHER NOISEMAKERS

Some of the cracking noises you hear when you explore the underwater world of a reef are made by shrimp as they click their claws or mouth parts together. You must look closely to find these tiny, brightly colored shrimp nestled among the tentacles of sea anemones. The shrimp wave their **antennae** back and forth to attract fish that have parasites clinging to their scales. In this symbiotic relationship, the fish get a good cleaning and the shrimp get a good meal.

You may also hear grunts *(Haemulon flavolineatum)* and squirrelfish *(Holocentrus rufus)* making raspy noises and grunting. *Why* these fish make such sounds is puzzling, but biologists can guess *how* they're made. They believe the fish make their **air bladders** vibrate or use bony parts in their throats to produce noises.

antennae
> movable sense organs on the head of a shrimp, crab, or lobster; also found on insects

air bladder
> organ inside fish's body which regulates fish's ability to float or swim at different depths — The bladder fills with gas to create more buoyancy, or floating ability.

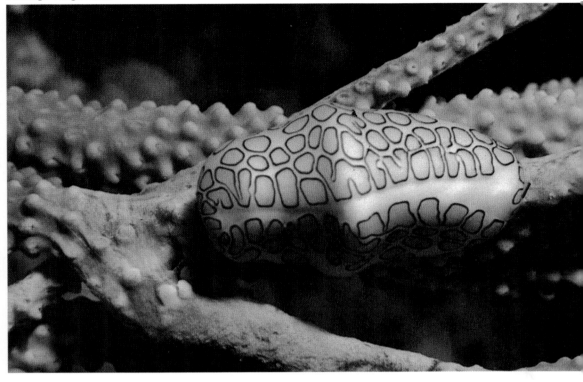

The flamingo tongue *(Cyphoma gibbosum)* lives by constantly munching away on the polyps of soft corals called sea fans *(Gorgonia ventalina)* and sea rods *(Plexaura flexuosa)*. The chiton *(Lepidochitona liozonis)* protects itself with strong suction and an eight-plated shell.

MOLLUSCS, OR SNAILS

A snail with a leopard skin? Try touching the flamingo tongue and watch this **mollusc** pull itself back into itself. The dots disappear and you see only a cream-colored shell.

Another mollusc loves to eat the spiny creature called the sea urchin *(Diadema antillarum)*. The helmet shell snail *(Cassis madagascarensis)* has a thick, muscular foot that can crush the sea urchin's spines in order to get at its soft, **edible** parts. The big beautiful shell of this snail is often found in shops. Unfortunately, collectors have taken so many helmet shells from the sea that there aren't as many around as there used to be.

The chiton is a strange-looking snail that clings to the underside of rocks along the shore. Trying to remove a chiton from its home is almost impossible, because this mollusc creates a strong suction between itself and the rock. Super suction, combined with eight overlapping plates gives the chiton a very good protection system.

mollusc
    animal that makes its own shell for protection
edible
    good for eating

Basket Starfish

White Sea Urchin

Echinoderms have spiny skins. In fact, *echinos* means spiny in Latin and Greek and *derm* means skin. This bristly bunch includes sea urchins, starfish *(Oreaster reticulatus)* and sea cucumbers *(Astichopus multitidus)*.

ECHINODERMS

Sea urchins, with their spiny skin, are surely echinoderms. These creatures may have short spines or long ones. The black long-spine sea urchin is a common **hazard** to snorkelers. If you happen to get a spine in your skin, you should leave it there. The spine is made of calcium carbonate, the same thing sea shells are made of. It will dissolve in about ten days while your body absorbs the calcium carbonate. Do not try to pull or cut out the spine because it will break. You risk a chance of infection if you poke and pull at it. See a doctor if it becomes swollen or very painful.

In turtle grass beds near reefs, you may find the sea cucumber, an echinoderm with a strange way of defending itself. When attacked, it spits out its insides. Then the **predator** is attracted to the stomach while the sea cucumber crawls away to **regenerate** its lost insides.

hazard
  danger
predator
  animal that kills other animals for food
regenerate
  re-grow — Most echinoderms can give up parts of their bodies and then *regenerate* the lost parts.

Bluehead Wrasse

Soldierfish

Four-eyed Butterfly Fish

Marine biologists aren't sure why coral reef fish have so many different colors and patterns. Color seems to have useful purposes: warnings to other fish, **camouflage**, visibility to mates, display of differences between males and females, and imitation of other fish to deceive predators.

COLORFUL REEF FISH

The color of the four-eyed butterfly fish
(Chaetodon capistratus) helps it survive. A black band
hides its real eyes. Two false eyes are located away
from the head. If a predator grabs at the false eyes, it
is less likely to injure the fish's **vital organs**. The false
eyes also confuse a predator, because the fish appears
to be swimming backwards.

The coloration of the blue-headed wrasse
(Thalassoma bifasciatum) means it's a supermale. He's
different from other male and female wrasses which
have yellow and white stripes. Only the supermale has
a blue head. He **courts** one female, while other
wrasses **spawn** in groups. The blue-headed wrasse
mates about 40 times a day.

The soldier fish *(Holocentrus rufus)* is bright red.
Many biologists believe this **adaptation** makes the fish
more difficult to see at night.

camouflage
    coloring that helps an animal blend into the background
vital organs
    body parts such as heart, brain, and lungs, without which an
    organism cannot live
court
    attempt to attract in order to mate
spawn
    form of mating in which female fish deposit eggs which are later
    fertilized by males
adaptation
    changes or adjustments that take place in animals over many
    generations and which allow a species to survive in certain
    environments or conditions

Many fish on a coral reef set up a territory and defend their boundaries. A tiny fish may try to chase a snorkeler out of its territory. Would this barracuda scare *you* out of its territory?

FISH WITH BAD REPUTATIONS

Barracudas *(Sphyraena barracuda)* are large, silvery fish with flashy teeth. Some divers fear the barracuda as much as the shark. But barracudas are only curious. One may come right up to you, circle you, or even follow you as you swim. This is scary for a **novice** snorkeler, but the fish's ferocious reputation is greatly exaggerated. It's usually not a hazard.

Moray eels *(Gymnothorax moringa)* also have a reputation they don't deserve. The moray is not poisonous and it doesn't attack. But if you put your hand near its mouth, a moray eel will defend itself by biting. You should never stick your hand into a coral crevice in case a biting fish is hiding there.

The moray has a snakelike appearance which may frighten you. It also opens its mouth to pump water over its **gills**. This gives the impression of an animal baring its teeth to attack.

novice
    beginner
gill
    organ for getting oxygen out of water

Royal Gramma

Red Coral Shrimp

The only way to view the coral reef at night is to get an underwater light and head for the water. During the day, the reef is full of bubbles and gurgles. At night there's an eerie difference.

THE REEF AT NIGHT

At night the reef may seem deserted. Some fish have buried themselves in the sand for protection. Others hide in holes in the reef. If you look closely at small things with your underwater light, you'll be richly rewarded. In the light, sea creatures look strange and brightly colored, and you'll see some that come out only at night.

Fish that **school** during the day are often found alone at night. Some fish, like the blue tang (*Acanthurus coeruleus*), change their patterns. During the day, the blue tang is bright blue. After dark this same fish adds white bars to its body.

The red coral shrimp *(Rhynchocinetes rigens)* was thought to be very rare until marine biologists began diving at night. They soon discovered that this shrimp is the most common one on the reef.

school
　　(verb) to move about in a group; (noun) group of many fish

Snorkeling is an exciting sport for all good swimmers who have had expert instruction and several hours of practice. You must be 16 to learn scuba diving.

ENJOY SAFELY

As in any sporting activity, safety is very important in underwater exploring. Begin snorkeling by following these steps:

1. Learn how to swim. (Consult with the Red Cross, YMCA, YWCA, or swim school.)
2. Take a snorkeling course.
3. Buy good snorkel gear, not toys.
4. Practice, practice, practice.

After you reach the age of 16, you can become a scuba diver by taking lessons from a qualified instructor at a diving school, college, or the Y. (See page 7 and Glossary.)

Whether you snorkel or scuba dive, reef exploring rules are:

1. Never snorkel or scuba dive alone.
2. Plan your trip and take first aid supplies as suggested by your instructor.
3. Know your limits and don't take chances.
4. Protect yourself from sunburn by wearing a T-shirt or put sunscreen lotion on your back and legs.
5. Choose safe areas and avoid boat traffic.
6. Avoid fire coral and sea urchins.
7. Remember a reef is fragile and needs your care.

Just as beautiful land areas are set aside in national parks, many reefs are now protected in marine parks.

MARINE PARKS

As you enjoy a marine park, you learn to care for the natural wonders preserved there. You're asked not to collect or damage any of the corals, sea fans, shells, or other animals. Spearfishing is not allowed.

What *can* you do in a marine park? You can take underwater pictures to record your adventure. Or you can become a fishwatcher. A fish guide book with waterproof pages helps you learn to recognize many species. You can watch different behaviors, feeding, cleaning, courting, and defense of territories.

Here are some marine parks where you can enjoy coral reefs or other underwater treasures.

- VIRGIN ISLANDS NATIONAL PARK, St. John
- Buck Island National Monument, St. Croix
      Box 7789 Charlotte Amalie
      St. Thomas, U.S. Virgin Islands 00801
- Channel Islands National Park (No coral)
      1699 Anchors Way Drive
      Ventura, CA 93003
- John Pennekamp Coral Reef State Park
      MM102
      Key Largo, FL 33037
- Fort Jefferson National Monument
      Box 279
      Homestead, FL 33030
- Biscayne Bay National Park
      Box 1369
      Homestead, FL 33030
- Great Barrier Reef Marine Park
      Australian Tourist Commission
      Distribution Center, P.O. Box A-1
      Dept. 254-028
      Addison, IL 60101

Coral reefs are important because they provide homes for millions of fish and other sea life. They also protect many coastlines from **erosion** and create gleaming coral sands for beaches.

REEFS IN DANGER

Many of the world's reefs are in danger. Oil spills and other forms of pollution can kill coral and destroy a reef. Other dangers include fish traps placed near coral reefs. They trap predators in the reef's food chain and upset the balance of life on the reef. Colorful fish are often caught in traps and wasted, because they aren't good for eating.

Marine life is endangered by the commercial collection of tropical fishes, shells, and corals for sale to pet and gift stores. These animals should be left in the sea to perform their important roles in the coral reef.

For thousands of years, the world's coral reefs have been washed by gentle waves and lashed by the fury of hurricanes. But can they survive the presence of people, their work, and their play? How much longer will colorful fish dart in and out among corals, sponges, and anemones? Perhaps you and others who care will make sure that reefs are preserved. Someone must provide your great, great grandchildren with the privilege of exploring and finding the treasures in the earth's coral reefs.

erosion
wearing away of sand, soil, or rocks, by wave action, rain, or wind

GLOSSARY/INDEX

F, 15

Fahrenheit; nonmetric temperature scale with freezing at 32° and boiling at 212°

filter, 25, 27

to strain or trap food from the water

food chain, 5, 45

the order in which organisms in a community feed on each other, beginning with plants, eaten by plant eaters which are eaten by meat eaters that may be eaten by larger meat eaters

geologist, 5

scientist who studies earth's history as recorded in rocks and formations

gill, 37

organ for getting oxygen out of water

hazard, 33, 37

danger

lagoon, 17

shallow body of water between a narrow strip of land and the shore

lime, 10, 11

calcium carbonate

marine, 5, 16, 26, 27, 42, 43, 45

of the sea

marine biologist, 19, 29, 34, 39

scientist who studies plants and animals of the sea

mollusc, 31

animal that makes its own shell for protection

nomenclature, 19

standardized names given to plants and animals by scientists, usually in Classical Latin or Greek

novice, 37

beginner

nutrients, 13

things that help a plant or animal grow or repair itself

organism, 21, 25

any living thing

oxygen, 15

element present in air and water; invisible gas needed for life

parasite, 21, 29

organism that takes nourishment from another living thing

photosynthesis, 13

process by which plants use light, water, and CO_2 to produce food

polyp, 5, 11, 30

wormlike animal whose secretions form the hard surface of the coral

predator, 33-35, 45

animal that kills other animals for food

prey, 11, 23
   animal caught and eaten by another animal, or predator
producer, 5
   plant or animal that creates food
qualified instructor, 7, 41
   usually a person trained and certified by one of the national associations such
   as National Association of Scuba Diving Schools, Professional Association
   of Diving Instructors, or National Association of Underwater Instructors
regenerate, 33
   re-grow — Most echinoderms can give up parts of their bodies and then
   regenerate the lost parts. See page 33.
salinity, 15
   saltiness
school, 39
   (verb) to move about in a group; (noun) group of many fish
scuba dive, 7, 28, 40, 41
   to swim under water with self-contained underwater breathing apparatus *(scuba)*
   which includes air tank, regulators, mask, and gauges
secretes, 11
   pushes liquid through the surface — An organism pushes liquid through its surface.
sediment, 17
   solid matter that settles to the bottom of liquid
snorkel, 7, 15, 17, 21, 28, 33, 36, 37, 40, 41
   to swim with mask, breathing tube, and fins
spawn, 35
   form of mating in which female fish deposit eggs which are later fertilized by males
species, 18, 43
   living organisms which have special features that only their group has
stag, 19
   male deer
surf zone, 19
   area where ocean waves break and form surf
symbiosis, 13, 29, 43
   relationship between two organisms in which each benefits from the other
tentacles, 11, 23, 29
   armlike extensions that capture prey
tropical, 15, 45
   located in the tropics (near equator)
turtle grass, 9, 33
   flowering plant that grows in shallow water and forms underwater meadows
vital organs, 35
   body parts such as heart, brain, and lungs, without which an
   organism cannot live